The Plurality Of Entrances

Leigh Zaph

Copyright © 2020 by Leigh Zaphiropoulos
All rights reserved
Printed in the United States of America

Cover photo by Stefano Guerrini / www.guerrinistefano.com
Author's photo by Bryn McCornack

No part of this publication may be reproduced or transmitted in any form or by any means electronic or mechanical including photocopy, recording, or any information storage or retrieval system without the expressed permission of the author, c/o Soualiga Press, P.O. Box 416, South Beach, OR 97366

Author's website: www.leighzaph.com

PUBLISHER'S CATALOGING-IN-PUBLICATION DATA

Names: Zaphiropoulos, Leigh, author.
Title: The plurality of entrances / Leigh Zaph.
Description: South Beach, OR: Soualiga Press, 2020.
Identifiers: LCCN: 2020920097 | ISBN: 978-1-7359364-0-6
Subjects: LCSH American poetry--21st century.| BISAC POETRY / General.
Classification: LCC PS617 .Z37 2020 | DDC 811.6--dc23

Published in the USA by
Soualiga Press
P.O. 416
South Beach, OR 97366

for Bryn and Scott

Acknowledgements

My gratitude goes to four friends, past and present, who've helped me with my desire to write. They are Scott C. McKee, Allen Foresta, Archie (A. R.) Ammons and William Asnis, each being an invaluable advisor and thought provocateur. Scott, in particular, has offered me continued support and advice since my return to writing, and this collection is dedicated to him along with my wife, Bryn. Also, I'd like to acknowledge with much appreciation the guidance I've received from Eileen D. Donohue who's helped me uncover and navigate much of the content found in the following pages.

Contents

Chapter 1: Suspected Novelties

Mentee's Lament	3
Senescence: To, And, From	4
Pontificating Ad Homonym -- Part 2, Or..., Johnny Snaps His Gum	5
Singing In The Drain	6
André Unperks The Coffee Klatch And Not Without Some Pounding	7
One Bridge, Two Views	8
Grist To Fodder	9
Ms. Lonelyheart's Advice To The Forewarned	10

Chapter 2: A Nervous Splendor

Coming, Too, A Head, Near You	13
Affairs Proved Counterfactual	14
Playing It, Covalently	15
Some Ins And Outs Of Talk And Breathing	16
After Ides	17
Redux At 65	18
Accounting For A Change In Handwriting	19
"Ladies And Gentlemen...The Beetles"	20

Chapter 3: Some Danceable Boleros

Do Anti-Metaphors Imply?	23
Historicity and Morning's Dream	24
Two Questions (from Ithaca, In Briefs)	25
Propped And Ready	26
Directing (every which way)	27
Downhill Racers	28
Nocturne	29
To His Bored Mistress	30

Chapter 4: Releasing The Reins

Revisiting The Watchtower	33
18° 2' 17.45" N, 63° 5' 51.18" W	34
Some Things To Be Avoided	35
What Comes As Best Should Have No Walls	36
Circumnavigation Finds The Origins Most Dear	37
Losing difference	38
Sharing In The Lunacy	39
Temp-O-Rary	40

Chapter 5: Dancing For Eels

Full And By	43
Teenage Musant Neo-Freudian -- Affected Type	44
Falling Out Of Range	46
Mausoleum: The Thirty-Eighth Ballad	47
Parodying With The Stars #2	48
I Got Her (Your Sister) Sick By Talkin' 'Bout Eating Some Purple Berries	49
Poetic Paranoia -- Part 2	50
Pantoum	51

Chapter 6: Riding Where the Tracks End

Devices	55
Nice Try	56
...And Another Thing:	57
Puntificting Ad Hominem	58
More Pungency Precedes Postmortem's New Revival Part 1	59
A Whorfian Hypothesis	60
Better Get Them Appleseed In The Ground, Johnny	61
Speaking Of This Briefly	62

Chapter 7: Eight Petitions Sighed By One

Carpe Diem Misapplied	65
Releasing The Reins	66
Recycling Waste	67
À Père Lachaise	68
Words That Merely Point	69
Panoplies Un-Privatized	70
10 More Quatrains-The Apothecary's Song-Translated Without Rhyme	71
Pablum Qua pablum	72

Epilogue	73

"...what can I make it mean."
—*Harold Bloom*

Preface

Conjunctive to this arid sense of normalcy,
the theme seen here is autobiographical:
segued from synaptic hide-a-ways,
papered fore Alzheimeresque dispersion,
hoping that some third dimension's
pressed within the vellum,
brought to live beyond the shakeout.

This impossible child of conscious burdens
as if death's whistle's being heard
before its lips are pursed.
Both outweigh the rest
to advocate the cause of immobility—
something that's immovable
whose consequence is only felt
by choosing to run into it.

Filled with visual reeking
to look in its direction is
to look no other way;
lost is north and south, east and west
when such displacements measure change,
and change defines the time,
the element of life, my life.

How am I to travel?
"Modify the sense of God,
and happiness will be achieved."
Who said this? I said this,
a statement made to imitate
the rope that's used to hang
the murderers of words.
And the lines, the lines of my digressions—
the lines of each regression—
merge the apple to the orange, to love
for anything that's spherical.

To wake and hear this hypergraphic tome scares me,
and just to know where my youth was after all
posits all in hypertexed display.
And though it's not
what I was put here for,
and not my job or outward function,
it is the sum that pushes keys
to open up a box still stuffed
and in the making—
a porticoed romance
that keeps me on my toes,
like twins.

The Plurality Of Entrances

Chapter 1

Suspected Novelties

"And tomorrow ends up no longer like tomorrow."

—C. P. Cavafy

MENTEE'S LAMENT

Memories and their death
is life's cruel joke.

    Both, once joined,
    become a final shadow (so they say),

cast with no light present
(if such can be believed),

    and then...
    they're truly, truly, truly (gone)[3].

All else converts but consciousness (the soul?);
and every thought left unexpressed

    remains, without question, unasked—
    lined up for quick demission.

This pike of lost cognitions
has no exits from its path—

    the heat behind its clench,
    the jaws that hold positions.

For us and those who take the place
of us and those, like words,

    possess the life of seeds,
    the chance to gnaw the air

    and minds that trip from day to day,
    or day to page, today, or rest what seems at night.

I see the cat beside me;
her slow wink knows the business.

The cat's a numen's radio,
I think it's time to listen.

SENESCENCE: TO, AND, FROM

I don't know when it started:
this quiddity that moved from
passion to a passive longing,
still spruce, but redefined.

The loss of winking hard
once drawn within the body's glances,
the chimes of thought
whose churning spelled as if
from rough veneers...
they both,
when asked for cause (and simply put),
re-mined the mind with answers.

The allegory's real, for once
there is no rope to tow on other spheres;
truth is truth is truth refined
to yield what's whitened, whispered—
seeking out mismanaged ears
despite that knowing sound, once found,
is not the same
as action.

Or then again,
perhaps this is a squall of sorts,
different orders,
tried,
and through these many bids,
trying,
a last attempt to excavate
those jungles started years ago.

Some answers seem to question this
from values raised
by ceilings now in view:
can retrospects eclipse unwelcomed dotage?
These values, are they well informed for any
who ignore past days
and then assume some other ways
a newer self-involvement?

Even in these grayer times
these fascinations take that name.
Each restive need to chew some nail
of discontent is not of our own making,
but then, and yet,
marked as this night's guest,
we take the role of regulars
with hymns and yarns to spin.

For any unaware, or at a loss
when coming to right angles,
we are the fruit for analogic thinking—
the anti-statisticians
whose hands are not for counting
but rather to be counted,
and made to aid these folds that sleep
beneath each false arrival.

I think I understand it now—
the meaning of egress,
the how, and why, it came to be,
and when   to be   applied.

PONTIFICATING AD HOMONYM -- Part 2, OR..., JOHNNY SNAPS HIS GUM

What isn't here
     concerns me:
          those foreign can'ts
  that implicate
         lost tethers
   from the living.

A pride of words (outside)
         converses, too,
   save a few
      to rest upon some obscure tomes
  re-pulsing now,
       to beat beyond our ears.

And still
       the reds repair
   to flush each page
        with rage, or shuttered eyes;
   or sound that sort
        by frequency.

     "Un-hand me, Sir!"
This clique of checks is heard
         but barely for the bettor
    who knows some gains
   are sums to come
       from losses by the others.

    And this is life.

   Beyond this plea's horizon,

   the vest of death's remains.

SINGING IN THE DRAIN

"In that case, what is the question?"
—Gertrude Stein

Their voices, born in concrete,
shine as glassy phantoms.
Moon and faces seam the light
for me to pekid thoughts adhered,
but willed as still
                          impalpable.

All eyes report
their own existence—
genomed, unique, they vivify
each change within a universe
whose values set as factual,
but hollow as a child's balloon.

And yet, some valid imageries
move slower with the coming cold;
flake by flake
uniqueness dies
and lets the lesser gaps expand
as scribbled, blearied, rationings.

(This interloping rubs nearby
a terror lacking fiction;
reality depletes all stores
of every other breath to be,
and this—it takes
my breath away.

I must forget

        to find some bliss

                before the whittling's done.)

"Dig the -- mostly uncouth -- language of grace."
—Geoffrey Hill

ANDRÉ UNPERKS THE COFFEE KLATCH
AND NOT WITHOUT SOME POUNDING

"The formula must die!" he said.
"A life that's based on fission is...
no life for any after all."

(And shudders could be heard,
 banging.)

"Poets should be ghouls,
digging up what's dead,
or soon to be; so know,
complicity's what can't recall
what death or limbo yields."

(But yielding couldn't be heard as yet,
 just spoons, and worry stirring.)

"True, the sums from you,
were for the stakes that forged returns;
And so I say, abandon all those ships!
A storm is threat'ning!
Prehend this resurrection—shout out:

Up with the kites!
Restart the heart
to lose the old refrain...
eliminate the strain!"

(And then one saw their pain,
 and it was very good.)

ONE BRIDGE, TWO VIEWS

I

And so it creeps,
sprung as leaks in consciousness,
and yet, my vision's fine,
but please don't hold me to it.

Know it (should it come);
if not, it's best to flee—
depart this land
where schooling's done
and dissonant,
like sudden insults found in songs, or rather
       placed in songs.

But still my point is just
like being redefined,
    waking with a will,
        which weaned from lessons, follows—
        welcomed like a cooler wind
        revered in hotter times,
                its this, that I believe.

But nonetheless, it creeps,
stinging leaks with consciousness,
its thought's morose viscosity.

And time, it always lives and breeds
beyond our own, storing rust
from all those missions
up to now,
      gathered,
          left,
              to drifting,
thinking:
    each is without need
               to be,
  —or exiting this stead—
           any
           longer
           cared for.

II

But you,
mistaking fur for feathers,
call for contributions
(and death's deceived—
its ownership secedes
when placed on night's horizon,
night,...and love).

The length and breath of phrasing measures
just the need for simple planting;
the love for *we* makes leaps,
generous with its whip of froth
and amplitude—
its intercepting interludes
unfalsed by your reception.

These interims of fine and flesh
are but one pulse in nature.
Taking turns,
we float to what's a side
for now and worth repeating,
tied to harbored dockings,
held by mooring's glory.

Wide-eyed we know

God is good;
and god is good,

too.

GRIST TO FODDER

to Rod Serling

*"You've got some 'Star-Spangled" nails in your coffin, kid.
That's what they've done for you, son."--Richard Brautigan*

The stares that empty history
are still thoughts unconceived.
A cloak (and shroud) of coarse design's
made-up for easy seizing—
    propelled by patent passions,
    braced by growth's momentum.

Choice is thought immobile;
the rush, a feeler working;
danger's heat is misconstrued
as sparks where fires are racing—
    shuttering a knowing scent
    from so much blood in stasis.

It's calling.

    War for war
    is made for toys;

        And also boys
        come play,
        to go this way of elms.

MS. LONELYHEART'S ADVICE TO THE FOREWARNED

Again I'll say:

all one writes's
two worlds away—
a mind in masterbation.

And more I'll say:

each subject's till
is best when uttered
self-described.

    Anticipate...
               more anticipation;

    tame each stance;

    excavate
            the gravity of yearning;

    find the tension
            relaxation brings;

    know to use all echoes first
    (for obvious reasons);

    sense some hidden hinge exists....

Seeing life's a moment
shows what's left's undone;
thoughts, if being cast unmet,
give out to chill the future—
drafts of blankness, whirling.

And dying?
it's just a final effort—
avoid it if you can (like rain).

And all of this
it must be done
while knowing, too.

And knowing, too:
your life is your umbrella,
someday left behind.

Chapter 2

A Nervous Splendor

for Bryn

"...my blood approves, and kisses are a better fate than wisdom"

—*from* since feeling is first *by e. e. cummings*

COMING; TOO; A HEAD; NEAR YOU

Rather than my lover,
It's my tête noire
That comes in the night.

Beside me, she (my lover),
    —for sure alloyed by the slick pollution that rides
    my constant words of questionable origins—
Must listen to me shuffle
Inside the tiny shack
That is my mind.

Beside her, me (myself and I)
    —looking through the shack's only window—
Finds my self surrounded.
I swing its squeaky door
And charge out puns blazing.

Or, when it's not a shack,
My cabin's on a ketch
    —my mind floating and wailing at sea—
But still, it's the same—
My sails find their lift (a drag for her).

I try to move, listening for
The homonymic, echolalic, fuckingly coprolalic
Foghorn that will guide me
To a bright lighthouse
(or rocks, she says).

It's a difference of opinion.
My hyperbolic ways carry me towards two axes;
She shouldn't be afraid—they're unreachable.
"It's not fear," she says, "it's boredom
And your inability to focus,
On me."

AFFAIRS PROVED COUNTERFACTUAL

Her sigh,
a breath with rope—
taut for future grappling—
finally left the plot.

What seemed to be a knot
became a braid instead,
and then a pulsed brocade
of lavender and eyes—
soft with less persuasions,
pale as Mengs' pastels—
a guide to knowing more,
like hearing foreign songs.

The harmony we scouted, took turns
to speak against the metronome
of early life's fixations—
Its tone: a sweet preamble
          to the moons that were to follow;
    and fun was in the tossing,
    the shifting in reverse,
    the taste for cloistered air...

Such commoness seems solely owned,
and like a joy once given,
stays in frequent play;
each day is on a wave,
the foam..., it never settles.

PLAYING IT, COVALENTLY

A cliche's plight
not unpracticed in the way of it
best describes her festooned motions—
those mast-propelled unevenings
that break from past's partitions.

What hangs for me from age (and left)
is seen and counter-fanciful,
a boutineer
whose endless use
turns florid scents to gravel.

And what is there to do? what to do:
she cannot know
my mind without a language,
my sake
without its latencies,

And yet she gives me license,
reality and other models,
a set to decorate,
another whirl at casting new cliches...
Oh boy!

SOME INS AND OUTS OF TALK AND BREATHING

The bone is back,
    one of many,
a breath about
    the lists of prior flights.

Tongue and lung admit
    retortion's take on provocation,
a workaround
    for pending respirations,

done with hope
    to win,
to whip it up,
    to word it good.

Perhaps it's time to listen, too.
    The warp of sound and air,
in linear rotation,
    gathers notes

to sing about
    its author's oscillations.
Orchestrations
    feel the rush

of pump and oxidation,
    brought in time
by two well-practiced
    bellows.

And when the next transpires,
    strikes the chords
to ride some newer sound
    with loosened reins,

the course is blunt
    and sharp from earlier themes;
reciprocation's dropped
    to favor soul desires—

those standalones
    beyond some curtseyed implication,
ready to be kissed
    and more.

Exhalation primes this pump;
    reduction brings no contradiction;
lungs are squeezed to make more room
    for you, and what comes next.

AFTER IDES

It's not you...,
          the cold inferno clocks forward from its hazing,
  the chasm lifts
               to set each spectrum's care
                                 (absent sighs)
               and blessed by color's new vibration
                                     prizing.

So honored...,
         the younger heat repeats
                            to cancel winter's stains
          like numbered embers,
                  crossed by greener sense,
                  then sanctioned for eclipsing.

And turquoise stays
               the grays and browns
                         of lesser, copper days;
  the clamp of cold discards
                from movement's inner friction.

Shadows un-sustain
                beyond a mumbled provenance...
            against a brighter hue...

Or is it you?

REDUX AT 65

"On ne voit bien qu'avec le coeur. L'essentiel est invisible pour la pensee." –Antoine de Saint-Exupery

Is this love?
I think yup.

With round my new meridian;
And brown my older color;
And sight a blurry festival
Of carefully draped verbena—
Ending early;
But Pounding like above...

"I am too old," I say
(faking it?);
"It's time
To rise and shine
This silvery apple," I say
(claptrapped, again?);

But zounds:
We are two wild and crazy
Kid's in love;
And gosh!
The sun will rise, again
(it's dawned on us)—

I think we're dew;
I sing.

ACCOUNTING FOR
A CHANGE IN HANDWRITING

for Eileen

Three trees are watching;
constellations, seen,
between the branches, peer.

A man below/beneath
looks at himself;
his self has little left,
or right,
or parked beyond his vision…
(e.g. like knowing that).

A woman here, too senses;
and by that sense
(for otherwise),
her eyes affix
to fathoms yet unmeasured,
as if it were her job
(as well as her protection).

The man cries out
for what in silence lies:
not knowing all;
but still
the woman feels
a sense of fear
for then, and when
her soul has seen too much.

But now, their minds,
once dark with words that cleaved,
now cleave them both to what remains,
and lasting—
a template faced with hope,
expressed,
and also paced with asking.

"LADIES AND GENTLEMEN...THE BEETLES"

"Nothing is so difficult as not deceiving oneself"
—Ludwig Wittgenstein

An alternate version:

we talk;
i say,
old girl
"what's this?"
you say
"what is that?",
meaning this,
meaning meaning.

our words are memories—
memories: memories;
shall we share
these thoughts
(with salt)?
yes!, that's it,
it tells me
so;

and so
you know:

she loves me,
yeah!
yeah?
yeah!...

we talk;
i say,
old girl
"what's this?"
you say
"what is that?",
meaning this,
meaning meaning.

our words are memories—
memories: memories;
shall we share
these thoughts
(with salt)?
yes!, that's it,
it tells me
so;

and so
you know:

she loves me,
yeah?
yeah!
yeah?...

Chapter 3

Some Danceable Boleros

"Don't look at your feet to see if you are doing it right. Just dance."

—Anne Lamott

DO ANTI-METAPHORS IMPLY?

for Scott C. McKee

With older latitudes discharged
immortal sense retreats like doubtful plans.
In its place we find an open field that asks
    what road is used when all is not
    like cold inside the sun's bright core.

Celestial reference is apropos—
presenting its own infinity
to show we're somewhere else;
    and on this day, and in this field,
    we see a dance as dance.

The twirling forms take the shape of better beings;
the waving grain quotes the wind
which born of sun, too, quotes back
and gives the world a new gospel,
with music playing
the great animator.

Beneath this ground of freshly found fertility
we find (or could)
the bones that moved to earlier beats
then went a waning way
but not their own—
defiant, acquiescent, doing both, somehow.

It's on this field with palette that
I try, I swear, to paint
to please those there,
    both old and young
    (or new).

I know my canvas well;
it holds a tree and leaves and canopy...
and I know too, about the dance
    that is a dance,
    and only that.

But once complete I find
my landscape seems as clouds to many
and wonder, is it me
or is my brush to blame?
Or did I simply miss the clouds
(look up, that is)?

If so, the many are the artists here.

We go again together
to see the dancers dance once more
and watch the latest gospel fall,
like meteors.

HISTORICITY AND MORNING'S DREAM

Forget the typewriters,
these monkeys speak volumes!
Each on its own pedestal, remains,
jabbering sense-filled theorems.

The mirrors are surprised:
forgetting duller likenesses
they now reflect a present way,
un-awry, and clear.

Unconcealed, discoveries
need not be named
to find their source or meaning.
Each point can pierce a child's mind,
pop out a laugh, or write a smile.

And what the older knowers know
is just the "term," if you insist;
and stay away from even that,
the anytimes you don't.

The greatest pleasure,
like the taste of orange,
flies among the label-less, revealed—
unriddled from the white that's borne
between the names, already struck,
and joys we've lost by naming them.

Don't stick to plans
or feel the heat that argumentum bring:
those double sides
that seem adhered,
when only one is needed.

Overthrow the rulers
of what's been left to measure,
they're like some frayed barometer
that only shows one pressure.

Reject the wrappers and their Logos;
find the end where thought's not only catalyst
for deeper thought—
is this the truth? Or death as some would say?

Aphoristic algorithms,
life's stock in trade,
life's twofold existence,
are better left inconsequent
within this poly-folded world.

Fear not oblivion,
it's what's been here before,
experienced,
and then forgotten.

Remember the monkeys
(they really are so cute),
forget the typewriters
and the lexiconic zombies
scratching at our door asking,
"WTF, are you surreal?"

For those of us who don't compute,
life's a fountain.

TWO QUESTIONS (from ITHACA, IN BRIEFS)

The here and there of it
implies a certain fullness,
a rafter holding court
and prospects
bobs, and yet
the reveries for less endure
the bluer notes
that sound it out
and testify
against their own disfigurement,
over,
and over,
and over...
And what's internal has a chorus
bridled by those hoarse emotions,
marked by unexpected seizing,
a tempered lump,
a life that's halved—
or so it seems—
while worry walks with all teeth ready.

Too early for returns,
it's Ithaca,
and not a coming back—
there are no suitors to be killed,
nor space for busy histories
to harry with their sake of linear lessons.

And there I stand,
before the waffled words
enforce some sign for competence—
the picture seems so clear:

    I see the vortex like a dog;
    I hear my master's voice;
    it rises out the weaker side;
    a megaphonic ego's there;
    a kind of inside outs the point:

        to draw and see the centre;
        to see the texture, hearing:

        the needle is religion;
        the record is its God;
        the player's on a table;
        the table's on a floor
        (just one of many).

Who build the house?
Who made the earth it rests upon?
...or are they just accounted for.

PROPPED AND READY

to John Wheelwright, or is it Keith Douglas

When players start to act,
And actors start their play—
Befuddlement begins.   You see

What each one thought was left—
Becomes stage right;
And what was right's
No longer right.

The lights, that were behind their backs,
Appear before them now, loudly.

Their eyes feel the breath
Of a thousand unseen faces,
Assembled to be entertained,
Convened to judge them, too;
And there's the rub.

Their performance,
Now clearly known as such,
Looks to Method, and the way
To bring the seated ones to rise
In fervent adulation.

If they can sing, they will,
If they can dance, they will,
If the new found script
Demands a slap
Or says to kiss,
They must.

(And what each one thought was right
Becomes stage left
And what was left is...
No longer left.)

DIRECTING (every which way)

to John Keats

Uh, listen, please:
first dodge each wave
of ranked duplicity
and moral ballast staying—
unreadably
sub-merged.

Note the later joined—
new thoughts embarked
with private lives,
leaving us
a group
of unearthed wonders

(Perhaps like God(s),
Before the aether,
Before our animation,
Before all sense of ripe existed,
Before those fascinations
Brooked no look upon themselves,

Which is to say
Before the water found its motion—
That first mirror
Housed beneath
A not-so-bright
But primal morning.)

Please know it's you
who has the power, too:
be powerless, grandly;
make hay with this
that helps and hurts you most,
then shelving it...move on.

DOWNHILL RACERS

We wake up each morning
skiing downhill fast,
unable to vadel.

Each time, we see (for us)
a doubtful destination:
        a chalet full of happy people
        drinking Irish coffee,
        laughing loudly,
        wearing sweaters,
        all that stuff...

We're ready now
to congregate,
but then again

(said hokelessly):

The Trees.

NOCTURNE

Caught in meaning's stubbornness,
this evening of blue stars is done
with what belies their interstitial way—
seeming then as whites, against a darker blue.

Our eyes perceive each
instant's tint and tabulation,
scored upon our own sweet life
as prefaced by a lesser source and fiction.

Pure sight is senseless—
my explication for what's seen
is unseen as unlimited,
and knowing all as being just a part.

But interjects aroma's thoughts,
enticements, and withdrawal,
soaked with joy—what middles bring—
with pulsed participation...

Surprisingly, the night's now new
with hintful aspirations;
and senses mount
the musical
that sings the songs
her set of wings will bring.

TO HIS BORED MISTRESS

Tonight, I find, the language is the land;
Its ancient belly's soul
Feels firm-like under foot—
Or so it seems.

But outskirts drop to find
A rising tide of contradicting sighs—
A luster in one's ears—
If truth be known.

And...,
What of this truth-like earthly tone
Of mental provocation?
And why such seasonality

When reasons come
To play upon
Our need for future's paradise
And facile fabulations?

Behold, I see a church of words
And other ghosts within our dreams.
How could they be as such,
When what once lived—their past—

Didn't come to us,
Nor did their death,
Or deathlike likeness,
Improvised.

There seems to be some foolery
And doubleness, again, I hear—
A surrogate for senselessness
Both here, and there, and more.

I'm right
I think
I'm right;
But saying it

Does drop me to a minorness
And onto life's most other quills
Of spine-ful fear and foible
(Embarrassments for me, (and you?)).

I'll grant, there is another way
But heavy with fake rectitude
And other fist-filled fantasies...;
So watch me dear,

Though chained to pillars left and right,
I'll stand and pull all down
To what there lies on up above
The whats you thought were tops;   Or...

If you prefer,

We can just sleep together.

Chapter 4

Releasing The Reins

"I am interested in language because it wounds or seduces me."

—from the Pleasure of the Text *by Roland Barthes*

REVISITING THE WATCHTOWER

"...poems are deflections."
—*Sylvia Plath*

And still,
the palm murmurs
a rare tune,
one of many—
without end,
and without end—
no edge
nor pine
for fear or grieving.

Unlike the mountains' piracy,
flung up and slant,
quiet stands—or better, rides—
on flatter turf—
a simpler mount—
whose rider turns
to softly whip
on through
to kill the span.

Hunger, too,
makes its naked inquiries:
what's being fed?
but not so much
as who has done the feeding,
or,
who's being fed (to make it clear),
as food has got no panic
to it.

Forget that now;
don't you see the cough ahead
when eyes must shift
from verbs to nouns
and death becomes their adjective.
How lucky to have been.
Oh God, I'm losing you.
Oh god.
oh shit.

18° 2' 17.45" N, 63° 5' 51.18" W

"Wrap us and lift us; drop us then, returned
Like water, undestroyed, —like mist, unburned…"
—Hart Crane

There is no loss in being overturned;
with brightness for the blood re-raised
but with no center, really,
these auras turn to halos.

Re-tributing with prior ordered lightness
to time, and placed
within its grasp
—some sift for older meanings—
like salt, it finds the tongue
and draws,
then voices nature's reel.

The sea blocks out the gnaw
—the yield of weathering latitudes—
snapping awes for source and signs
that flock with fears of otherwise.

The wind rewinds its motions
rimmed by stronger skies' transparencies,
while knowing sides—that nab the neck—
take on their others' aptitudes.

Sails here do the selling,
now and too,
they draw the eyes to heft-less hours,
peaking new adventures to tack the rising partnership
of man and sun and wind—
a course, reverting from its clichéd status,
wondering less complete
but holy In its quest for mirrored likeness…

And all this brakes
an urban take
on what's tradition's tide:

> *Confusion slides and waves*
>   *(from pendular emotion),*
> *then fathoms safer levels reached,*
>   *to carry better parcels;*

> *stretch awhile…*
>   *there is a different market, here—*
>   *brighter cloth and redder fruits*
>   *to unsheath time's remainder.*

SOME THINGS TO BE AVOIDED

This gallery portends
a metronome of beasts--
re-annotated visibles
impulsed from past expletions.

Each canvas seems a word
that rests just north of sound,
and moving south of better routes,
forgets the walls have rules,
(and hooks beneath what's visioned).

And hung beyond the grasping,
the rasping of some early days
(missing),
notes the fingers taking turns
to crease or do some sleeping--
as agents of erasure;
                          by erasure;
                                          for erasure...
(bitter's angels, really).

So light the candle, bastard boy,
push each key that's marked as chosen;
toggle just uneven times
to liberate what's frozen.

WHAT COMES AS BEST SHOULD HAVE NO WALLS

to Roger Bacon

Once felt, death's a sole demand.
Leeward bound, eyes make clear:
Devices have their say to self,
And mind's the mind's best leader.

The times that saw false ecstasies,
Opacities, that wrote all else,
Couldn't edify confusion as
The source In need
            of deep remission.

Whose fragments, tilled as tethered bits,
Spilled forth like organs from a dog,
Beside the road,   and dead;
Its horrors felt outside—
Since inner fears
Would be too clear.

Whose rousted spines—
Electrified from knowing such—
Did compromise with curtain calls;
Unending,   sending
Matters lost,
Like keys
Within the brain.

So still, the sake is plunged,
And like a jaw that's opened,
Consumates post-birth, reheard,
to start the next new epilogue.

Why?! The epigraph was clear—
forged for finer circumstance:
a word before the words,
whose etiquette and manners shown,
             and flowed out unfinessed!

What?! Apparently, the voice,
Without an accent to the ear
(since heard from birth),
Was easy to ignore—
A flaw within man's nature:
To seem beyond his true address!

If life had eaves
To help us see
What lies beneath,
We'd know these tries
Are ricochets,
And not toward something
Better.

CIRCUMNAVIGATION FINDS THE ORIGINS MOST DEAR

for Sharon Olds

Why disguise the manner's aspiration,
to take the venture's glide among
a pride of froth-filled frictions
is to be as one as two to peal
where frontal meets excursion.

And hammered tandem bliss repairs
to join a quantum need
for finding pleasure's ancient ward
and life in living's bout against
all mindful interference.

(And wordless triggers shout aloud
in flush and fretless unison—
the world's at play,
its length till change
is like a mineral's life.)

Humanity is estranged from its authentic possibilities."
—R. D. Laing

Losing difference

is finding all the stories of the world:
    the matrix met unwoven,
    the mystery caught exposed,
    gliding white as recomposed
        i.e. all colors merged,
    and errors best forsaken, too,
    unborn, like birth itself's
    unborn becoming—no—
    as always having been
    the realest pleasure (home)—
    the place to be, (like Paris in the '20s).

What is to suffer
    canvasses
    an all-to-common
    unrevolting yet:
        the oldest thinking scapes
            ignored,
        the speaking gut of verbs
            ignored,
        and verbs portrayed as nouns
            implored
                to still this spike's confusing blast.

What is can only be
    affinities,
    drifting out
    (it's true)
    but onward toward
    a greater largeness.

It's simply losing difference
that finds
the stories of the world
and you,
a greater aspect.

SHARING IN THE LUNACY

"When full,
the moon's a stare,
that pulls the mind and water..."
—from Sharing In The Lunacy *by Leigh Zaph.*

Our eyes
from apprehension,
pillowed
from the dark
(especially that night),
gazed upon
the round's bright cast of replication.

The waters rose,
sinking minds
to rest in near submersion.
Confined to just a spit,
they jutted out to sea's reality
which felt (to me) ungrounded,
then wholly drenched by blue sensations.

The taste of surf was woven there
(and too, for you) in briny saturation;
the thread was real,
explosive in its pounding,
breaking to the sound
of closet thoughts that clung unseethed
from lack of light's exposure.

But in that night,
beyond the rooted land's packed sanity,
the choppiness made waves for us
that reached our inner scenes
of breach and wary consciousness,
deadening the dryness there,
too honed and milled with reason.

It was this moon in absolute
which phased us on reflection;
its transportation's legacy
remained beyond the dipping;
and what was caught through increments—
the solar backing's flash in play—
removed the dim

of all the nights
before.

TEMP-
O-
RARY

And this,
the first to be
written
(by me)
is murder in the mind—
A different matter,
palled by mine own sanity
as sanctified
by we who see
repeating beats
as gift.

And self,
it skirts
self death
upon each word
of lost occurrence—
one event
as precedent
to none or fading innocence,
played for who remains
for you
what carries out
old hearts of choice
and better conscious weeping
(like the willows
 spread about,
 and just
 before the clearing).

Chapter 5

Dancing For Eels

FULL AND BY

to T. S. Eliot

But
He has no need to talk

To you, he is the sailor
                      who departs—

Not to go to sea,
            but rather,

                          leave the land
Alone,

      and out there.
                  Who,

When sightings reappear,
Sees each empty rock as proof

The mermaids don't exist,
And any songs they may reserve

Are cadent of a lonely life. They chant
He should listen,

                ...or that's the plan.
His plan

Is to leave the land,
To keep himself busy in the rigging

Looking at the line between what's blue
And darker blue

                for something else.

TEENAGE *MUSANT* NEO-FREUDIAN -- AFFECTED TYPE

for Dad

In 1961, I read Dr. Theodore Isaac Rubin's *Lisa and David*. A few months later the movie came to town, its title transposed for phonetic reasons I suppose, or *pour les raisons anciennes* (if you get my meaning). In the movie, Kier Dullea wrestles his demons for over an hour, (seven years later he'll wrestle HAL the computer, but for much less time, and in a much longer movie)... But I digress. On this particular afternoon I enter, with stealth, my father's office; he's absent, "how more not, than often" (*je pense*, cleverly). I take *his* place behind the couch, sit in *his* chair, grab *his* pad and with less guilt the Montblanc pen I gave him for Christmas. I lean back, pen to mouth, eyes to ceiling, still too young to have a beard (or jaw cancer), but ready, yes, ready to begin, *vraiment prêt*. I hear (i.e. "imagine", if this helps you), a knock at the door; it's my dear aforementioned colleague, Dr. Rubin. "Why Ted, do come in, please have a seat," I say, "and allow me to illuminate... here's what you may have missed: [*allegrissimo*] I've thought about Lisa and must say it's my opinion that the main basis of her behavior is due to a lack in ego development and the secondary process associated with it. The images in her mind cannot be applied faithfully and accurately to the objects found in the external world. She's psychologically undeveloped and unable to identify, with any degree of stability, her images with an appropriate external object. Being unable to proceed normally, she has regressed to an infantile stage and the inadequate primary process which offers no effective method for forming accurate mental representations of the real world. She has, for all practical purposes, lost all sense of reality. For example, the lack of ego development and therefore of an ability to produce concrete object relationships is apparent in Lisa's attempts to create external objects out of internal ones such as parts of herself: the splitting of her personality--Lisa and Muriel--and the separation of her hand from the rest of her body--with the hand moving autonomously--and even these as objects can only be maintained temporarily. I see Lisa's regression as being easily observed in her self-cuddling, jumping, rhyming and sing-song behavior. I would even go so far as to say her hiding in closets represents an obvious attempt at complete regression to the prenatal state. Though I see other examples I'm not sure why her ego development has not taken place but I can suggest a few theoretical answers such as the possible instability or unavailability of objects around her in her early childhood, or even a diminishing ability for object-cathexes.

As for David, the problem seems to be due to the development of a poor psycho-sexual identification. Because of the apparent lack of sexual discrimination between his parents who do not sufficiently display the characteristics typical of their respective sexes and social roles, David's Oedipus complex has remained unsolved and his castration fear practically reversed. At the same time I feel his ego has been unable to cope with the complexities this situation has produced in the resolution of his bisexuality conflict. In essence, he doesn't know if he is a male or female (as expressed in his reaction to the sideshow hermaphrodite). This confusion is accompanied by anxiety, causing within him a fear of his own body and a wish to become separate from it. This wish is reflected in his excessive intellectualization which he uses in an attempted to become a disembodied brain and can partially explain his phobic reactions, too. By being touched, he is made aware of the existence of his body and thus his confusion and anxiety. This fear of touch is also due to a parallel set of difficulties arising, again, from poor psycho-sexual identification. It is probable that early in his life David's sexual and aggressive impulses fused, and his young and immature ego was unable to cope with these combined impulses except in a repressive or suppressive manner. Since the ego was incapable of doing this indefinitely, it became necessary for the punitive superego to take over. It's this development of the superego that accounts for David's obsessive and paranoic traits. As applied to his phobia: if he is touched, it arouses within him his sexual-aggressive impulses and the superego must intervene in a punitive manner. Paranoia, whether it is directed towards a person or a concept such as time, is similarly explained by the presence of the superego, which unlike the ego, appears to the person to be a force outside of his mind. I could go on but you get the picture. [*andante*] "You're right of course," Dr. Rubin utters, standing up to leave, "and please do say hello to your Dad for me, you smart and worthy son, you; and my best to Mom and Sis." (he's clever, too). After he leaves I grab a peanut butter and jelly sandwich and turn on the TV. I see George Burns turn on *his* TV, saying, "Let's see what Gracie's doing..."

FALLING OUT OF RANGE

Our language was the cat that chased its tail.
Through apertures, her face revealed her mind:
A bungalow, as keen as keen inhaled,
With pleasing rooms to spend our words in time.
But time then changed its meaning from its rhyme
To match the cause of desert's shift and sand;
Life's fading till, affixed to lost sublime,
Showed stiffening, and swelling forms unplanned.
Now, the plain remains, fields of vacant land,
An aging home propped up with broken frames;
And fate's a rope that's breaking strand by strand
Where all's been pilfered of its early aims.
No bending's here where once there was a gust;
No winds remain before the coming dusk.

MAUSOLEUM: THE THIRTY-EIGHTH BALLAD

for Hans Magnus Enzensberger

H.M.E. (1929-   )

Thank God
(rhetorically)
he wasn't born
a score or decade sooner
inflected with
a massed accord
unfathomed and
six million deep.

From then
he speaks with contra-
diction,
or remnant costs re-served,
       as founded how
       in difference
       with what survival asks,
            enjoining Hymns
            through writing time
            among the rest with flowers—

     "Ach, wen vermögen
wir denn zu brauchen?
           Und jene, die schön sind,
O wer hält sie zurück?
Eines ist, die Geliebte zu singen. Ein anderes, wehe,
jenen verborgenen schuldigen Fluß-Gott des Bluts.

     Dann erst kam der Tänzer,
immerfort anders auf alle des Gleichgewichts
schwankende Waagen.
     Sein Aufgang ist Dasein, beständig
nimmt er sich fort und tritt ins veränderte Sternbild.

Hiersein ist herrlich,
dieses heißt Schicksal,
und so drängen wir uns und wollen es leisten
-Weit." *

* cento drawn from Duino Elegies by Rainer Maria Rilke

Parodying with the Stars #2 (of Stevie Smith's *Not Waving but Drowning*)

NOT MOANING BUT YAWNING

Nobody heard her, the woman wanting,
But still she lay sighing:
I was much further from what you thought
And not moaning but yawning.

Poor lady, she always loved coming
And now she's just lying
It must have been cold for her so her heart gave up
Trying.

Oh, no, no, no, it was this cold always
(still wanting, still lying)
I was tired with desire all my life
And not moaning but yawning.

An analexi with apologies to Crosby. Stills, and Kantner

And upon my father's death

I GOT HER (YOUR SISTER) SICK BY TALKIN' 'BOUT EATING SOME PURPLE BERRIES

For six or seven weeks
the water grips us;
horror, and this foreign land
ships one thing: you are leaving.

If you smile (you don't)
we might laugh again
(everybody does)
'cause that is something

we can have—
the same language,
the way it's supposed to be, once free,
and where a fair wind will—

blowin' warm
out the other side—
tell me (my friend), go, be;
go, and keep us both alive.

Please, then, let us say
I've been away,
your wooden hand
on my shoulder.

Anguished as we watch you die,
people understand
you know
you probably don't need us.

Now, you're free, easy
(very easy);
cries coat your echo,
far away.

By your leaving, I can take over,
(we haven't got the
need to know of who
won).

I see there's silver in us all,
at the shoreline,
from everywhere
we are.

Can the course I'll set lead on?
South of a guess,
it's just very me,
and (aaaah, yes) easy:

all I can do
is stare as
human feelings die
from them.

POETIC PARANOIA -- Part 2

Without a trope, what's left need not imply;
Taken at its words, life's long sentence seems
Mad-libbed from out, and not our own reply.

These interfering minds that come as teams
Confuse what faith could form within each head—
To live with comfort, and our mental means.

Left alone, we'd hear our own being said
And know, what is, has come from sacred hearts—
Their past, and future's thoughts, as yet, unread.

It's just not right what's made, and what departs;
The origin of fear is likely here
As too, the senseless loss this thought imparts.

Such interjects have brought me wear and tear;
I want you all to simply be not there.

PANTOUM

for Bryn

The man in blue waves;
His mind is made up.
The cats, worried, eye
His trembling hands.

His mind is made-up
With trembling blue arms;
His trembling hands
His hand to her heart.

With trembling blue arms
The blue woman holds
His hand to her heart—
The past is unseen.

The blue woman holds
The man in blue waves.
The past is unseen—
The cat's worried eye.

Chapter 6

Riding Where The Tracks End

"Philosophy ought really to be written only as a poetic compression."

—Ludwig Wittgenstein

DEVICES

to L. J. J. W.

These robber words,
the rooms they flock and fabricate
(as exitless, no less),
these false reported prophesies,
hollow as a feather's bone
infest the slowing sphere—
a world of spinning tops,
cocked and thrown but once,
their string a chanced divinity
for having been at all.

The point of movement is
to miss the point of fear,
and phrasing's vision—
to gyrate in a shadow
brighter than its caster,
to see the brownest beauty in
a leaf that's deaf to sun;
to "See the world aright"
   (or disciplines capsized),
to roll the faux components called expression—
the digital lie
whose ring deprives the feeling of its soul
and flags the death of real,
the birth of corpses,
the minions drawn behind.

   (Do crystals match the one within?
   Do meanings have their orders?
   It's been suggested
   work occurs outside the conscious,
   that sharing's done through resonance,
   and resonance, precessing.
   Suggested, …just not stated.)

NICE TRY

Obsession levies,
and what's heard
must be clear
in order to be heard,
or so I'm told... BUT,
such merit badgers me
and lacks the words
now uninvented,
its space is merely brought by wind
and proclaims each entitlement
before our hearts are written,
and what is written has its own
recited death to lead—
and minus proof or fancy
stands
between what's you and
what's no longer you.
Listening, the songs arrive delivered
by a bright-filled night's physician,
and day's apocalyptic tenor.
Scenery's impersonation
strives all action
caught behind,
fabled, fraught, and fucked,
and cycling through
what's rest and morning's madness.
And then this foolish folio
of what each river's bank reveals
through placid visitations,
drawn from higher sources' morning mists
and clouds convincing quota,
beckons (now there's a word)
to it's origin's pretense
for meaning without surplus,
and jamming out the possibles
of stepping out,
outside...   the nerve!

...AND ANOTHER THING:

What is this state (affairs aside),
this realm of fragments still but borne
by populist demands for swifter planting...
whose clustered spores re-germinate
the hoax and screed for poorly placed geographies?

Which destinations, left for us, are found inside these lists of
pocked atrocities, false hope, and vision's halo ossified?
(The cataracts that lie within are motionless and cold;
while kindleless, and left alone, all fires must stay unstarted.)

Whose false accelerations—goal-less in their aspect
like a vortex caught within itself and of itself, repeating—
fall upon the strictest entropy's arrival—
its ceaseless sword of normal sepsis, unadorned,
but sheathed inside a paste of jeweled reality?

And what each one needs to wear's a crystal node,
a spiraled atom's rosary, a painted sweeper orbiting
through fractal distillation's choice of sight,
and placid life's true centers;

And all is seen and set aglow in search of crest's curation.
It's said the exposition starts   tomorrow.

PUNTIFICATING AD HOMINEM

for Ricky Jay

What's manifest
has a dialogic rhythm,
unpacked
but still unaltared.

Its call's a door,
the early space's walls,
its sealing's clear retreat
stops complements unspoken.

Markings wind the vane's direction,
healing vapor's missed,
dry and tightened chords resound—
forging voices heard, allowed.

Brought in stages, fazing's haul,
claims to sum the running whole,
seaming with an attitude's
pared and false confection.

So woe is me, and woe to them
and taut constriction's principals
who after all in latent swarms
are best when left unborne.

MORE PUNGENCY PRECEDES POSTMORTEM'S NEW REVIVAL Part 1

Troubled again
With what I saw,
There was a certain potency
In not dreaming;
And with the table set
To praise the Dead (a metaphor),
What was bred
From in and shrouded selfishness,
Retained a rush to serve
Diurnal's black plate special.

Knowing the real kidnappers,
My manikin soul discerned
What danced before each grave (not on)
And ether's questioned run
On-ground through hill
And dale capacities,
And other such suppressions—
Seamed with strings,
And strings of string—
A double sensed in feast.

Subtle as torn muscle,
Such commotion made the sun seem slight
By comparison
To what burns
Nearer's still in ghost-like
Fires
As sure
(If sure)
As man's distaste for ash,
And love for what it was...

(This ends part one's abruption
of older words from new;
let green and curtain drop
the lights down low—
above the masses—
for no one's here
to play the part of Lord
or understudy,
and the script to put it right
is clearly   undecipherable.)

A WHORFIAN HYPOTHESIS

Every effable duo seeds neurotic response;
Transitional acts call forth, demanding more;
Eden's language, if it was known, would offer confirmation
As true and accurate as each past's future was.

Leaping into others' minds,
We see our ex-positions for what they are:
Ambiguous certainties, corrupted understandings,
But rarely...serene venues inside life.

Beknighted nomenclatures rule this day, commonly;
Thoughts that worship words assure each mind full crisis;
For each spouse of reality (or chaos),
Such intercourse seems as others' infidelities.

Know, effective translation must make a leap, not merely reckon.
No, if left unused, can force the hand of locked, psychotic, ravings;
Yes and every gray will merge;
Love and hate...

BETTER GET THEM APPLESEED IN THE GROUND, JOHNNY

"...that in any case we speak only one language -- and...we do not own it...Let us make it say what it does not know how to mean to say, and let us allow it to say something else."
--Jacques Derrida

Unfortunately,
The meaning flows;
Awake is signified,
The day: its signifier,
Its sign: too many.

Its shape and conversations,
Rise in resonance unraveled,
And seize in stagnant fashion.

If overheard,
You'll find there's hell to pay,
As similes resist to say
What's really on their minds.

But sleep is my Cassandra,
And what's seen here
Is unbelieved by day,
And night's own piece defied.

This interim unearthed,
Dismantles old excursions—
Squares its sense to stay;

And lingering,
Actions out of tense like clay,
Seek a different imaging
And chance for art's display.

"You here!
You don't understand:
You build the next same structure
With sunless beams
To hold things up,"
Tried,   —again
In stagnant fashion.

If evanescence dreams
Of omnipresence,
What's asked
Is just
That we behave
As if a God exists,
Or other gods, instead, insist
We epigraph with moral acts
And reason without camouflage...

And if each turn
Seems cause for worlds to still,

And being hit
Accrues the sums of what was missed,

And what's unowned, too,
Is lost with owned, the same;

And unborn things assume
The newer role of never be,

And dryness steeps in greater dryness—
With voices gone, like light at deeper fathoms,

And matter's actualities
Seem parsed by what is absent...

It's then, I'll seek
To deconstruct
A sentence that's worth listening to
(and not some false cognation);
    'cuz certainty comes twice, my friend,
    and what's between could be, at end,
    a stare through fuddled water.

SPEAKING OF THIS BRIEFLY

for J. G.

she said
we've approached
the edge of understanding
(but from which side?);

she said
we use all parts—
and felt the need to say how,
(but here, again...
what end?);

I'm confused
she's confused,
I know I'm just a sound;

you?

i couldn't care less.

Chapter 7

Eight Petitions Sighed By One

*"The piers are pummelled by the waves;
 In a lonely field the rain
 Lashes an abandoned train;
 Outlaws fill the mountain caves..."*

—from The Fall Of Rome *by W. H. Auden*

"Everything not saved will be lost."

—Nintendo *"Quit Screen" message*

CARPE DIEM MISAPPLIED

for Al Gore, Jr.

The tides reveal a signal here and there,
   the air, a long but failing dynasty,
questions who or what is being nourished.
   History, with rust from past excursions

is not the history that's faced again,
   and this is new—a future set adrift.
Effusion from the shallows trumps concern;
   earth's dexterity slows and freezes.

The new decors of day are tarnishing
   a broken gift that cannot be returned.
Incapability, a false retort,
   braces for the present past, alone.

An unclaimed ethic fosters poison's birth
   and next return; and selves, wrapped up, just wear
the mask of otherwise and pursed excuse.
   Our wending has a risk's uniqueness to it.

The children of this current's child
   will lose the sites, and sights of clean array—
earth and sky, sun and moon—
   without an eye to see them.

RELEASING THE REINS

Seemingly,
direction—
the great diviner—
infiltrates as common thought.

Its march begins with aphoristic flairs,
too much obliged,
its source, too forced, from supraficial goosing—

       binding,
              blinding,
                     holding,
                             scolding—

all in linear defeat/fired by foreign heat.

Ever red, ears are pulled or pushed
(where eyes, instead, should lead).

Life moves forward, false pretensed.

Toward, in time will whisper next,
"I'm dying..."

And what ensues—futures, once invisible—
are, no longer [even] that.

(And should the subject turn to death,
 lousy with such reasons,
 eyes again (and here, make no mistake)
 can finally see, then canter off
 the mights, might disappears.)

RECYCLING WASTE

A moon away,
the sleeper's face
drifts like old mahogany.
Her eyes from time,
no more arrayed as sanpaku,
take each squint in stride
with what the shelf
of artificial means
purports.

She medicates with legs crossed,
her slip exposed, but uninviting
to her newfound kin, all caught within
the lexicon of chemistry's submission.

I know this place, I think,
as having been for me before.
Its different musts
dismay the breath of babies;
its fog of false combusting leaves
all that was, behind—
a faulty go at death's consumption.

And were it seen some other way,
unwedded to a moving frieze
of centuries' old blue sounds,
what billows forth is calm and clear,
(as is the end
to where such pivots first began).

À PÈRE LACHAISE

Each note assigns
a title to its berth;
each soul, re-plied by certain light,
resounds the dislocation—
the cleft from those
less mortal than ourselves.

The scene and breeze are constant,
unpressed but always pressing;
the soil that mounts
these bones in bins—
sarcophagi of older themes—
re-marks the separation.

One sees carved rhymes in search of cause;
but short of these,
the lilies sway
and speak with wordless motion,
their silence bends, then blends un-dinned
the lists of favored notions.

And know,
there is a certain growl within this hallowed hum,
a dry allure to help each notion cure
its taut convictions caught within the ear,
or still in full retreat,
...confused by such decay.

And not too few would have such secrets die
(now saids within the saying),
whose rubs are worth repeating,
whose truths could collate more within
the hinge of past to things which passed
from time, and by the living.

The sin of knowing less
than those who came before
may lead what's left to low degrees
that live within the waiting:
a cold that haws and stacks, as last,
the span of cautious leapers.

WORDS THAT MERELY POINT

Granted, there is no fleece,
but what's believed
or undiscovered's
worth a stumble.

See here...,
it's words that merely point,
and bless the literal array:
the festered stars,
(please know that they were forced),
the blocks for fading souls,
(please know that they were forced to stack).

Enough!:
All factories display
the product from those ancient wards,
the tablets that were written first
then gained immortal face
without relief, yet unerased.

And here...again,
our memories, like wheels,
spin each cell's assassination;
but shots that took so long
ago
shift
from hearth, to myth,
to anonymity—
my father told me this,
the rest,
I knew myself.

I wonder what the other fathers say,
uh, think,
er, feel.

PANOPLIES UN-PRIVATIZED

" "There must be some way out of here" "
—Elston Gunnn

A bird can too, perch otherwise—
feathered for the function,
just about to sing
with Mesozoic meanings
not unlike our own,
but flinched from being heard
against our fixed unwillingness.

A tree has function, too.
its phototropic manner gives a lesson:
how our eyes should listen:
use the light,
un-complicate the rest,
terminate our terror-tilled terrain.

Yet still, our minds,
once captured by the arrogance of words,
start their fake tableaux—
their frames of thought refreezing
any chance for feelings held
behind this black parade.

How is one to qualify
what's only quantifiable?
The moon's dark side's no different,
except when seen as such
and lost within that label—
hidden by some need for quick response...
and weight.

Falling to our knees
it's no wonder
we wonder
what comes next.

10 MORE QUATRAINS—THE APOTHECARY'S SONG—TRANSLATED WITHOUT RHYME

"qué le tienen hecho con el
jardín que fue confiado a usted?"
—Antonio Machado

"In the heavens, a fire is seen"
—Michel de Nostredame

The passengers
that filled our vision's field
are gone one hundred years,
passing us their reason:

End will come
to all who walk on echoes,
overlapped by present talk
to slaughter what's eternal;

Among the reeds that gallop from
a different wind,
conversation's lost,
enforced through other changes.

The distant line's
a cyclone, now,
and not so distant,
either;

The clouds rise up
from prospects' race
between what's time
and physical;

The worshippers
of knowing less
ignore the future's
knowing such:

The background's constant whisper,
the songs that should be
man's true love
(or unused, man's last widow).

Direction's being pulled itself,
toward plastic's
immortality—
a poke and lifeless remnant.

Man's new nature is a font
that's foreign to his mother,
rising in the smoke of burning cities,
ushered by his last renewal.

And on the outskirts, songs are being read
about the next implosion,
too few, here, listen to the few;
death will come in clusters.

Pablum Qua pablum

These words are spit,
flung with force and entropy;
what matters,
splatters unassigned,
and through the mouth
appends the rest to sadder tears,
unseaming me
from pleats and other gathered-fors.

It's hard to hear the rip
inside such soggy bits,
the blind can't see
the spattered neithers
        slung against
   the white, with fingers flipping
                        doors
                in quick surrender.

My hand has lost its grip,
and what it thought
it came here for:
to frisk its mate's prolixity for fictions still unwritten...

and after only twenty lines,

I see   that I'm   alone.

Epilogue

WAITING FOR THE Q & A
to Archie

Again, I'm sorry;
No travelogue for you is here;
No re-
considered radiance.

This scape has one,
but chosen, prefix: a lone
and soul-filled filament—
steeped in gray
and all that paints
a personal decor:

For one,
man's seen as broken
—redemptive options gone,
and earth, itself,
without ourselves
is hurt,
but free to go.   Yet still
with stills despite,
in search of doors and borders,
I enter just
with titles only,
stymied by each scalding *which*
and numbered less devotions.

    (And all what's felt
    is all that can't be said,
    like knowing shadows can't exist
    without some bright behind them—

        those long gray bands
        as roads defined
        by photons' motions casting,

        born from sun
        or other light
        but never seen beside them.)

And telomeres, once frayed, remind:
A private dusk is coming—

        so recognize the sovereignty
        of stones, and too,
        organic time
        as not enough to measure all
        or even fright's contention—
            to live to die
            that more might tour
            the earth by such successions...

And yet,
my whispers seem so loud and lasting,
but not as trees would have us hear,
they, who will remain,
injured yes, but winners first
and last to see the sun and its flagration,
    (beyond these woods where man once lived,
     and failed to make a clearing).

Is it best for us to know and yield our softer parts
and welcome life's reprisal:
    last words for days as brightly colored scars
    (that are no matter, really)
        echoing the us that grieve
        but know it's simply time to leave?

www.ingramcontent.com/pod-product-compliance
Lightning Source LLC
Chambersburg PA
CBHW051258110526
44589CB00025B/2866